CARI

• YOUR PET

HAMSTERS
AND
GERBILS

Don Harper

Published by

A SALAMANDER BOOK

Published by Salamander Books Ltd.,
129-137 York Way,
London N7 9LG,
United Kingdom.

© Salamander Books Ltd., 1996

ISBN 1 85600 058 3

1 3 5 7 9 8 6 4 2

CREDITS
Editor: Helen Stone **Design by:** DW Design, London
Colour Separation by: Pixel Tech, Singapore
Filmset by: SX Composing Ltd., Essex
Printed in Slovenia

PICTURE CREDITS
Artists
Copyright of the artwork illustrations on the pages following the artists' names is property of Salamander Books Ltd.

Wayne Ford: 6, 8, 13, 27, 39, 51(B)
Clifford and Wendy Meadway: 28, 29   Guy Troughton: 25
Photographs
The publishers wish to thank the following photographers and agencies who have supplied photographs for this book. The photographs are copyright of the photographer and have been credited by page number and position on the page: (B) bottom or (T) top.

Aquila Photographics: M Gilroy; 12, 18(T), 20(T), 26, 30, 32, 45(B), 46, 47, 51(T), 57, 61
Marc Henrie: 4, 5, 11, 14, 15, 17, 21(T), 23, 38, 40, 42, 48, 49, 52, 53
Interpet Ltd.: Bernard Bleach; 36 Adrian Turner Photography; 31(B), 36, 43
Cyril Laubscher: 10, 16, 18(B), 19, 20(B), 21(B), 31(T), 41, 63
RSPCA Photolibrary: Sister Daniel; title, Tracey Duce; 55, E A Janes; 24
David Sands: 34, 35, 37, 45(T), 58
Jacket photograph © M Gilroy, supplied by Aquila Photographics

Contents

Introduction   4
Hamsters and gerbils in the wild   6
Domestication   10
Hamster and gerbil behaviour   12
Choosing your pet   14
Questions and Answers   22
Choosing the right gender   24
Understanding your pet   26
Housing your pet   28
Fitting out a cage   30
Cleaning the cage   34
Positioning the cage   36
Questions and Answers   37
Feeding your pet   38
Grooming and handling   40
Letting your pet out of its cage   42
Questions and Answers   44
Breeding hamsters and gerbils   46
Caring for the young   48
Questions and Answers   50
Exhibiting your pet   52
Going on holiday   54
The first signs of illness   56
Questions and Answers   59
Care checklist   60
About my pet   62
Index   64

Introduction

Hamsters and gerbils as pets
With their friendly, inquisitive natures and cute, playful ways, both hamsters and gerbils make charming and delightful pets. They are easy to care for and, if acquired at a young age, they can become very tame and easy to handle.

Housing and exercise
One of the benefits of keeping hamsters and gerbils as opposed to other pets is that you only need enough space to house their cage, making them suitable for most homes. They do not need extra exercise, only gentle play and handling.

Feeding and cleaning
All pets need daily feeding and care and, if you are keeping a caged animal, you must also be prepared to regularly clean the cage and its fittings. But being a responsible owner is part of the pleasure of keeping a pet and following a routine of proper care will ensure that your pet is happy and healthy.

Bringing home a new pet
Buying your first hamster or gerbils is a big step and needs some careful preparation. You will need to have a cage or gerbilarium ready, along with food and bedding before you bring your pet home. Getting a new pet is always an exciting time for the owner, but it can be a stressful time for the pet. It is best to allow the animal to come into a calm and quiet household and be left to explore its new surroundings in peace for the first day or two.

● *Right: Both hamsters and gerbils make delightful pets which are lively and curious by nature. They become tame if handled regularly and it is possible for you to form a strong bond between you and your pet.*

Hamsters and gerbils in the wild

Hamsters and gerbils are both part of the rodent family. Wild hamsters are found in eastern Europe, the Middle East and Asia, and gerbils come from southern Asia and parts of Africa.

Life in the wild

In the wild, these rodents often live in deserts where the sun is scorching and dry during the day and the temperature can drop to below freezing at night. They make their homes by burrowing into the ground where they stay during the long, hot days and spend the cooler nights gathering food.

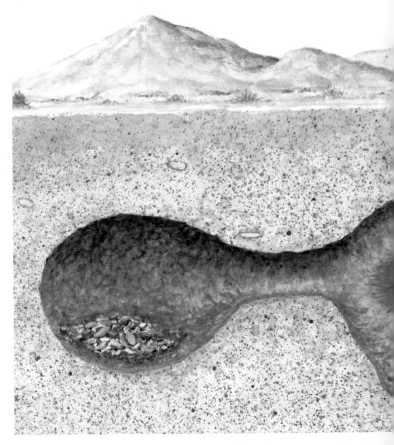

Feeding

Food and water are scarce in the desert and these rodents must search for seeds, nuts, plants and other food. Because water is hard to come by, these creatures have adapted to need only a little water and can survive on the small droplets of dew which form at the entrance of their burrows in the early morning.

● *Below: In the wild, hamsters burrow below the scorching desert where they make their home. These underground caverns offer protection from the soaring daytime temperatures and also provide warmth and protection during the freezing cold nights.*

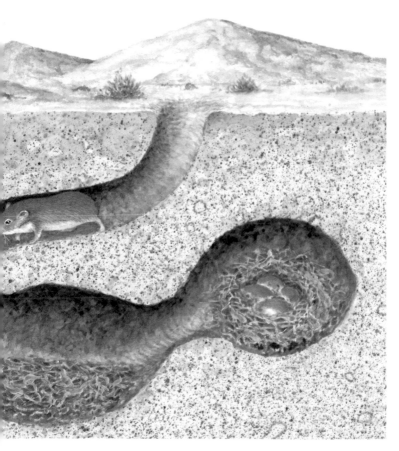

The Golden hamster

The Golden hamster, which is the most common pet hamster, originally comes from Syria in the Middle East. Very little is known about Golden hamsters in the wild, as they are not common. In fact, it is thought that these hamsters only live in a small area and could be in danger of extinction. They are solitary creatures and will only seek out other hamsters for mating.

Other types

Two other types of hamster have also become popular as pets in recent years. These are the Dwarf Russian hamster, which comes from the eastern area of central Asia and the Chinese hamster which comes from the northern part of China and parts of Siberia.

Mongolian gerbils

Gerbils have only been kept as pets for the last thirty years and only the Mongolian gerbil has become as popular as the Golden hamster. Gerbils originally came from Mongolia, which is a country in north-eastern Asia. They also live in neighbouring areas of Siberia and China. The summers here are especially hot during the day and cold during the night and in winter the temperature falls well below freezing.

Life in the wild

Very little is known about the natural life of the Mongolian gerbils. They are sociable creatures which live in colonies. They eat seeds, nuts and green plants and store food in special chambers in their burrows in the winter when there may be snow on the ground, making finding food very difficult.

Other species

A few other domesticated species are kept by specialist rodent breeders, but you are unlikely to find them in pet shops. The most common of these is the Egyptian gerbil, which is a reddish-brown colour and does not have a bushy tip to its tail.

● *Left: Unlike hamsters, gerbils are sociable creatures which live in colonies. They live in harsh climates and build burrows below the ground to protect themselves from the elements and would-be predators.*

Domestication

Golden hamsters were first seen outside their native Syria in 1880. Fifty years later, Dr. Israel Aharoni unearthed a nest of hamsters with their mother in a cornfield in Syria. Unfortunately, the female attempted to kill her offspring and Aharoni was forced to hand-rear them. He took them to the Hebrew University of Jerusalem, but their ability to gnaw was not fully appreciated and they escaped.

Modern pet ancestors

Four were recaptured safely and almost all of today's pet Golden hamsters are descended from this group. They became popular during the 1930s and 1940s and today, millions of hamsters are kept as pets all over the world.

● *Above:* *Although most of today's pet hamsters are descendants of the first Golden hamsters which came from Syria, Dwarf Russian hamsters and the Chinese hamsters shown here are becoming increasingly popular.*

● *Above:* Most of today's pet gerbils are descended from just one group captured in Mongolia in 1935. They proved to be easy animals to breed and today there are many different varieties including the Argente shown here.

The first domestic gerbils
The Mongolian gerbil was discovered in China by a French explorer called Pére Armand David. In 1935 Professor Kasuago, a Japanese scientist, managed to catch some live gerbils close to the River Amur in the eastern part of Mongolia. He took them back to Japan where he successfully bred them. Most of today's pet gerbils are descended from his colony.

A fitting name
The scientific name for gerbils means 'little warriors with fingernails' which is a fitting name for a creature with sharp burrowing claws.

11

Hamster and gerbil behaviour

One of the most important things to bear in mind if you want to keep Golden hamsters is that they must be housed individually. They are not at all sociable and will fight to the death. Introducing two hamsters even for breeding purposes needs to be carried out very carefully.

Gerbils are quite the opposite and should never be kept on their own. In the wild they live in colonies, and as pets they need the company of others of their kind. However, they breed easily so it is a good idea to start out with two gerbils of the same sex which come from the same litter.

● *Above: Both hamsters and gerbils need to gnaw to keep their teeth in trim. You should provide a gnawing block or some similar hard material such as nuts or hardwood for your pet to gnaw on, or it will begin to gnaw at the cage itself.*

● *Right: Hamsters have special pouches inside their cheeks which they use to store food. When the pouches are full, you will notice that your hamster has an unusually puffy-cheeked appearance.*

Gnawing

Wild hamsters and gerbils gnaw with their teeth as they search for food and, for this reason, their sharp front teeth never stop growing. If their teeth become too long, it becomes difficult for them to eat which can lead to starvation. Pet hamsters and gerbils will gnaw on any hard material to keep their teeth in check.

Storing food

These rodents have many predators in the wild, particularly when they are out of their burrows and above ground. Feeding times are especially dangerous and so hamsters have developed a safe way to gather food. They have special cheek pouches inside their mouths which go back as far as their shoulders. These allow the hamster to quickly grab as much food as possible and then return to its burrow to store or eat it in safety. These unusual pouches are responsible for the hamster's name which comes from the German verb 'to hoard'.

Playing dead

Gerbils have a worrying habit of playing dead, particularly if they are picked up suddenly or frightened by a loud noise. This is a natural reaction, as predators such as cats will not attack a dead animal. After a short time, your gerbil will come round and dash back to its burrow, lucky to be alive.

Choosing your pet

There is little difference between a hamster and a gerbil when it comes to general care, but gerbils do tend to live longer. They may live for four or five years, whereas hamsters rarely live more than three. Both can become very tame if you start with a youngster aged between four and eight weeks.

Hamsters
Hamsters are often less bothered by handling than gerbils, although they can still give a painful nip if you insist on holding them when they plainly don't want to play. Hamsters have been bred in over 30 different colours and several coat types so there is a wide variety to choose from.

Gerbils
Gerbils are often more active during the day than hamsters, although neither group is as nocturnal as their wild relatives. Both tend to be quiet during the

● **Right:** *Whether you are buying a hamster or gerbil, it is important to choose a healthy animal. It should have a lively and inquisitive nature and should have a clean, clear nose and eyes. The coat should be smooth and glossy with no sores or damp patches.*

day, although gerbils may bang their hind legs on the ground. This can be a sign of nervousness, but often shows anticipation of a regular event such as feeding.

Active creatures

Hamsters will not make much noise themselves, but tend to be more active on an exercise wheel which can be disturbing.

Choosing a healthy pet

Whichever you choose, you should make sure that the pet you are buying is healthy. It should have clean, bright eyes and the nose and ears should be clean. The fur should be smooth, glossy and even, with no obvious sores or damp areas. Although shy at first, hamsters and gerbils should be curious when introduced to anything new, so avoid buying one that seems disinterested or that skulks away into a corner when you approach it.

The Golden hamster

The natural colour of the Golden hamster is golden-brown with a white belly, but there are also both lighter and darker shades available. The Dark Golden is a rich red-brown colour with black hairs scattered throughout the coat and a grey belly.

Cream hamsters

Cream hamsters are very popular, with three different types to choose from. The Black-eyed Cream has a pure cream coloured coat. The Ruby-eyed Cream is lighter in colour, but you may need to see the hamster in a good light to see the dark red colour of its eyes. The Red-eyed Cream has red eyes and is far more common than the Ruby-eyed. The colour of the coats vary and some can be quite dark.

● **Left:** *The attractive golden brown coat of the Golden hamster has been developed through breeding to produce the wide range of colours seen today.*

Albinos and Whites

The flesh-eared Albino is a true albino with a snow-white body and red eyes. The Dark-eared White has dark ears, but it can take up to three months for this to show in a young hamster. The eyes are darker and the coat may have a yellowish tinge.

New colours

A wide range of colours has appeared over the last thirty years and are now quite common. The Honey is a yellowish colour with deep ruby eyes, and there is also a lighter variety called the Blond which has black eyes. Grey hamsters tend to be dark grey with slate-blue underparts and Black hamsters have a dense black coat. Other newer colours include the Chocolate and the Lilac, which is a pinkish shade of pale grey.

● **Top:** *The Albino hamster has distinctive red eyes and a pure white coat. The Red-eyed Cream (left) has a darker coat.*

17

Coat markings

Hamsters of all one colour are called 'self-coloured', but there are also different types of markings. The Tortoiseshell has white, yellow and other coloured patches of fur and there are also Spotted and Banded hamsters.

Different coat types

It is not only the colour of the coat which can differ between hamsters, but the texture too. Satin hamsters can be bred in any colour or pattern and have a very glossy coat. Rex hamsters have a rougher appearance than normal and slightly curly coats. The Long-haired originally came from America in the 1970s where it is called the Angora. It has a long, thick coat and is also known as the 'Teddy', because of its cuddly appearance.

Chinese and Dwarf Russian hamsters

Both the Chinese and Russian hamsters are smaller than their Syrian relatives and have fewer colour variations. The Chinese hamster has a distinctive dark streak running down its back and there is also a white-spotted variety. The Russian has a dark upper coat with paler underparts although the entire coat may become much paler in the winter.

● *Above:* The Chinese hamster is smaller than the Golden hamster and has a distinctive dark streak down its back.

● *Opposite top:* These Golden Piebald hamsters have coats which contain patches of the original golden-brown colour and white.

● *Opposite bottom:* This long-haired, Red-eyed Cream has a soft, fluffy coat.

Gerbil colouring

The natural colour of the Mongolian gerbil is known as the Agouti. There are black hairs in the golden-brown fur on its back and its underside is white. The tail is covered with fur and ends with a tuft at the tip.

Patched coats

The first new colours of gerbils came from Canada in the 1960s. These gerbils have white patches, often on the head or at the back of the neck.

New colours

In 1968, a white Mongolian gerbil appeared for the first time. Although it had pink eyes like an Albino, there were still some dark hairs on the tail. This type is known as the Pink-eyed White.

● **Above:** *The Argente gerbil has a pure golden coat with a white belly and is also known as the White-bellied Golden.*

The first Black Mongolian gerbils were bred in 1978 and these gerbils often show odd traces of white hair.

Argente gerbils

The Argente also appeared in the late 1970s. This has a pure golden coat with a white belly, which is why it is also known as the 'White-bellied Golden'. Breeding Argentes with Black gerbils created Lilac gerbils, and breeding with Pink-eyed Whites created Cream-coated gerbils. Grey Agoutis have also become common.

● *Above:* Patched coated gerbils make attractive pets and are available in a wide range of colours.

● *Opposite:* The Agouti is the most natural colour.

● *Above:* The Dove Grey was created by combining the Lilac and the White and has a paler coat than the Lilac.

Questions *and* Answers

Do any of the hamster or gerbil varieties need more care than others?
Long-haired Golden hamsters do need regular grooming to prevent their coats from becoming matted. If the fur does become badly matted, it is best to trim off the mats of hair rather than trying to brush them out. Tugging at the fur will upset the hamster and it is likely to bite you!

Is it true that the coat of a Dwarf Russian hamster changes colour during the year?
Some do. In the wild, a Dwarf Russian hamster's coat will become paler at the beginning of winter to act as camouflage in a snowy landscape. You may notice a change in your pet's coat in late autumn as it becomes paler.

Are Dwarf Russian hamsters more sociable than Golden hamsters?
Unlike Golden hamsters, both Dwarf Russians and Chinese hamsters can be kept together in groups, but you must watch closely for fighting. This is particularly important when they are first introduced or if they are breeding. Do not attempt to introduce a new hamster to an established group, as it is likely to be attacked.

Do the patterned coats of young gerbils and hamsters change as they get older?
No. The markings on a young animal remain the same as it grows. This can be useful in identifying a particular animal within the litter or adult colony.

● **Above:** *A Long-haired hamster will need grooming to prevent its coat from matting. A soft baby brush or comb is ideal for this purpose.*

● **Below:** *The Dwarf Russian hamster is more sociable than its Golden cousin and can be kept in small groups.*

Choosing the right gender

It is very important to know the sex of your gerbils so you can house them accordingly. A mixed group of gerbils may produce more youngsters than you can house or care for properly. Although hamsters are solitary creatures and cannot be housed together in groups, if you intend to breed hamsters at some point, you will also need to be able to tell whether your pets are male or female.

● **Above:** *It is important to know the sex of your gerbils or you may find yourself with too many young to care for.*

How to inspect a gerbil or hamster

When buying a first hamster or gerbil, the breeder or shop owner will be able to tell you which sex your pet is. However, if you are going to breed your own, you will need to be able to tell whether the young are male or female. This can be done by looking at their underparts. To do this you should hold the rodent up and look from below or place the hamster or gerbil in a container with a clear base such as a empty fish tank, so you can inspect it from beneath. Don't lay the rodent on its back as it will find this position distressing and it will bite.

What to look for

There will be two openings close to the hind-legs.
These will be close together in a female and further
apart in a male. Looking at a Golden hamster from
the side can also be helpful.

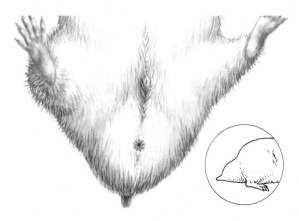

● *Above:* *The male hamster has a wider gap between the
two openings on its underside than the female. If viewed
from the side, you will also see that the hindquarters are
stepped down to the tail area.*

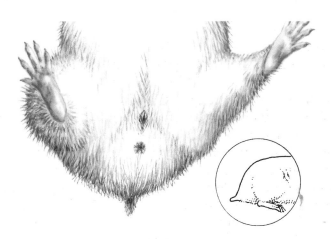

● *Above:* *The female hamster has a shorter gap between
the two openings and its hindquarters run in a smooth curve
from the back to the tail.*

Understanding your pet

It may seem odd that a creature which comes from the desert should be covered in a thick, warm coat of fur. But in the wild, hamsters and gerbils rarely venture out of their burrows in the heat of day and their thick coats are vital for keeping them warm at night.

● **Above:** *Gerbils will often sit up on their hind legs, using their tails to balance. This frees their forefeet for gathering food and feeding.*

● **Opposite:** *Your pet hamster may decide to hibernate if the temperature suddenly drops. To avoid this, keep the temperature as stable as possible.*

Storing fluids
These rodents are able to survive with very little water. They have efficient kidneys and pass little water. Gerbils in particular produce a very concentrated urine, and this is why they do not have the unpleasant odour that rats and mice do!

Sight and smell
Because hamsters and gerbils are burrowing creatures, they do not have strong eyesight. Instead they rely on their keen sense of smell. Hamsters have scent glands on their hips which they use to mark their territory.

Built for burrowing
Both hamsters and gerbils have powerful, clawed feet for moving earth. As pets, their claws may become overgrown and need to be clipped by a vet.

Safety in the wild

The wild gerbil has developed a clever trick to fool any predator which might be looking for a quick meal. A gerbil has a tuft of hair on the end of its long tail which can be used to distract the attacker's attention away from its body. When the predator pounces, the gerbil may lose the tip of its tail, but it will escape unharmed. However, this trick can only be used once as the tail tip never grows back.

Hibernation

Golden hamsters are one of the few pets that will hibernate if there is a sudden drop in temperature, especially if there is not much light. You should try to avoid this situation as your pet might not have built up enough fat reserves and could starve. Keep the room at a stable, warm temperature and make sure that there is enough natural light.

Housing your pet

There are three basic types to consider when buying a home for a hamster or gerbil: a standard cage, a glass or plastic tank, or modern tubular housing.

Metal cages

The traditional choice for a hamster is a metal cage, complete with an exercise wheel. This type of cage has to be strong enough to withstand its teeth and you should check for any sharp edges which may be dangerous. Choose the largest cage possible, preferably with two or more levels.

Ensuring the cage is secure

Some modern designs have a tough plastic base, but this must be covered with a mesh frame to stop the hamster gnawing through the plastic and escaping. You should also check that the spaces between the bars are narrow enough, particularly if you are keeping a small Dwarf Russian hamster which can slip through the bars of some cages. These hamsters are often safer housed in a converted fish tank.

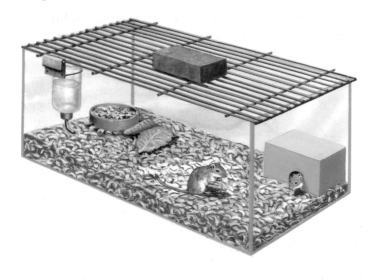

Tubular housing

Modern plastic housing systems have a series of tubes which connect larger living areas. Pieces can be bought separately which allows you to design your own housing system and add extra space for a growing gerbil colony.

Gerbilariums

Gerbils are best housed in a converted fish tank or a gerbilarium, which is a deep glass tank covered with a secure, mesh lid. This allows them room to exercise and to burrow.

● **Left:** *Hamsters are happy housed in a standard cage fitted with an exercise wheel. A large cage with two or more levels provides extra space for your hamster so that it can have plenty of exercise.*

● **Above:** *A gerbil colony is more suited to a converted fish tank or gerbilarium which should be filled with a thick layer of wood shavings to allow the gerbils to burrow. Additional toys such as plastic tubes will also be appreciated.*

Fitting out a cage

Sawdust or wood shavings can be used as a floor covering for your cage but these must be bought from a pet shop to ensure they are free from chemicals. Both materials are cheap and absorbent, although most gerbils will prefer shavings because they are better for burrowing.

Providing bedding material
Proper bedding material must also be provided. Meadow hay is a popular choice, but it shouldn't be damp or musty. Special paper bedding or cellulose fibres are good alternatives and cleaner to use. The bedding should be placed in the sleeping quarters or in a quiet, hidden part of the cage.

Avoiding danger
It is important to buy proper bedding material from pet supply shops. Other materials found around the home may seem suitable, but could prove harmful if swallowed by your pet. Some fibres can block a hamster or gerbil's intestines and newspaper ink can be poisonous.

● *Left:* A nesting box will need to be provided if you plan to breed your pets.

● *Opposite:* Wood shavings are the best lining materials for a gerbilarium.

Exercise wheels

Most hamster cages have a fitted exercise wheel. This should be either of a solid design or with only small gaps between the treads so the hamster cannot trap its foot as it turns the wheel. Hamsters will mostly exercise at night but, if yours seems to spend all day in the wheel too, you should remove the wheel after a few hours. These wheels are not suitable for gerbils, as their long tails may become trapped between the treads.

● *Below:* The safest type of exercise wheel has narrow gaps or none at all between the treads.

Food and water

You will need to fit the cage with a drinker bottle which can be fixed to the side of a hamster's cage or from the lid of a gerbilarium. Food should be supplied in heavy, straight sided pottery dishes which your pet can't tip over.

● **Above:** *Your pet must always have access to clean drinking water. A drinker bottle is the best way to supply water, but make sure a young pet knows how to use it. Choose one with a metal spout which your pet cannot gnaw.*

Gnawing blocks

Both hamsters and gerbils love to gnaw and will gnaw at the cage and its fittings if no other material is supplied. Hardwood branches or a gnawing block are useful for keeping your pet's teeth in check.

Suitable toys

Both hamsters and gerbils are active creatures and like to play, so you should provide toys for interest.

Ladders, ramps, branches and pebbles can all be added as can old mugs, jam jars, toilet roll tubes and flower pots. Avoid anything made from metal or with a toxic painted finish and never give foam or fabric playthings which can be chewed and swallowed.

Keep it simple

Don't clutter your pet's cage with toys. Two or three will be plenty at any one time and you can remove these and replace them with others from time to time to keep your pet interested.

● *Above: Curious by nature, hamsters and gerbils will enjoy exploring toys, especially those which appeal to their burrowing instincts.*

Cleaning the cage

Cleaning the cage regularly is important, both for your pet's health and to prevent any unpleasant smells in the room. Hamster's cages need cleaning once a week, although a gerbilarium may only need the lining changing and a thorough cleaning every three months. Every day you should remove any droppings and uneaten food, checking thoroughly under the bedding in case your pet has made a secret store of food.

Replacing the lining and bedding

You will need to house your pet in a safe temporary cage or tank while you clean its home. Remove the toys, fittings and food bowls and then tip the used flooring and bedding straight into a waste bag. If

there is sawdust stuck to the bottom of the cage, you will need to wash it out with a special pet disinfectant available from pet supply shops and scrub it if necessary. Make sure you dry the base thoroughly before putting down new lining and bedding material.

Water drinkers and food bowls

You will also need to wash out the food bowls, toys and cage sides or bars. Special disinfectant wipes can be bought which are easy to use and safe for your pet. The drinker needs regular cleaning to stop algae growing in the bottle. The water could also become polluted with bacteria which would be harmful to your pet.

The new litter

Avoid cleaning out a cage where a female has recently given birth, as scent is very important to rodents. Gerbils have a special scent gland in the middle of their stomach which marks their territory and they feel safe in familiar surroundings which have this scent. Placing them in a clean, sterile environment may cause the mother to abandon her young or, worse still, attack them.

● *Left: It is important to keep your pet's cage clean, removing any uneaten food and soiled litter every day.*

Positioning the cage

Your gerbil or hamster should be kept in a warm room where the temperature is likely to be constant. The cage should be stood on a secure surface where it can't be knocked over and kept out of direct sunlight and draughts which will be uncomfortable for your pet.

● *Above:* *It is important to position your pet's cage out of direct sunlight and draughts and on a secure surface away from any other pets such as cats and dogs.*

Out of harm's way

If you have other pets, such as cats or dogs, you must make sure that the cage is well out of their reach. Even if there is no danger of a cat getting into the cage, a hamster or gerbil will certainly be upset by a natural predator coming too close.

Peace of mind

These pets should not be kept in a room where you sleep. They are active at night and can make quite a lot of noise as they move around.

Questions *and* Answers

I have bought a three-tiered home for my hamster. Should I provide food and bedding at every level?
No, this is not necessary. Your hamster will probably want to snuggle down in the lowest tier as this is the deepest part of its burrow, so you should place the thickest layer of bedding here. Food need only be supplied in one part of the cage which your pet can return to when hungry.

I want to buy a tubular housing system for my hamster. What are the disadvantages?
These systems are ideal for young, lively pets, but there is always the danger that as your hamster gets older it may become fat. Larger hamsters have a tendency to get stuck in the narrow tubes.

● **Left:** *Tubular housing allows you to design a home for your pet. Plastic living chambers are connected by tubular tunnels which mimic the burrows that hamsters and gerbils make in the wild. Extra pieces can be added and changed around which makes it ideal for housing a growing gerbil colony.*

Feeding your pet

Both hamsters and gerbils are very easy to feed. The basic seed and nut mixtures from pet shops are ideal, or you can buy different ingredients and mix them together to make your own. You should offer one main meal of seeds and nuts in the early evening to last through until the following day and a selection of fresh foods each morning.

Seeds and nuts

Cereal seeds, such as oats and barley, are carbohydrates which give your pet energy. Peanuts and sunflower seeds have more fat and should be given in smaller amounts as too much fatty food will make your hamster or gerbil fat.

Many mixtures also contain biscuit meal, which may be coloured red or yellow and flaked maize, which looks like cornflakes.

Storing food

Seeds and nuts must be kept dry, or they will become mouldy. It is best to buy a small amount of food at a time rather than a large sack to be sure that it is always fresh. Old food can become infested with fodder mites.

Fresh foods

Fresh foods form an important part of a balanced diet for your gerbil or hamster. It is better to give a small amount of green leaves and fresh fruit and vegetables every day rather than large amounts less often. A sudden change in diet is likely to upset your pet's stomach.

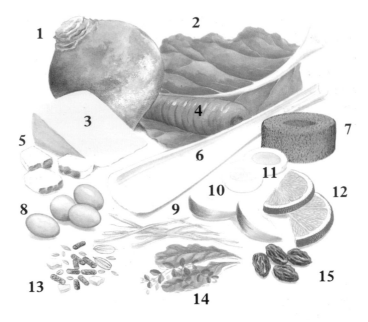

● **Above:** Suitable foods and gnawing materials for your pet include: 1. swede 2. lettuce 3. cheese 4. carrot 5. dried baked bread for gnawing 6. celery 7. gnawing block 8. grapes 9. grass 10. apple 11. hardboiled egg 12. orange 13. seed and nut mixture 14. dandelion leaves 15. raisins

CHECKLIST of food types

- Basic seed mixture in the early evening.

- Fresh fruit and salad such as carrot, apple, pear, grapes, tomato, lettuce, chickweed or dandelion leaves in the morning.

- Occasional treats of small amounts of mealworm, fish, hardboiled egg or cheese.

Grooming and handling

When handling any rodent, it is important to remember that they bite. Gerbils are less likely to nip than hamsters, but both are nimble creatures which will escape at any opportunity. When handling your pet, you should be careful not to let it fall as this could cause a serious injury. It is safer to sit down, kneel on the floor or stand over a table so if your pet does wriggle free, it won't fall any great distance.

Picking up your pet
You are most likely to be bitten if you attempt to pick up the hamster or gerbil without giving it warning. Allow your pet to sniff your hand first, so it can recognise your scent.

Taming your pet
Try to encourage the hamster or gerbil to step on to your hand, by holding it flat and encouraging your pet to move on to it, rather than gripping the animal tightly. When you want to move the rodent elsewhere, use your cupped hands.

Lifting a gerbil

Don't hold a gerbil by the tip of the tail where the skin is very delicate. It is better to encircle the base of its tail with your fingers, holding the gerbil's body with your other hand.

Grooming

Gerbils naturally groom each other and need no extra help from you. Short-haired hamsters are also capable of grooming themselves, but long-haired hamsters need regular brushing. Use a soft toothbrush dampened with warm water and brush the fur with gentle strokes away from the head. This should be done every other day to keep the coat in good condition and tangle-free.

● *Above* and *Left:* It is important to hold your pet correctly. Always support the animal's weight by placing a hand under its body, using the other hand to gently restrain it. Never hold a gerbil by the tip of its tail.

Letting your pet out of its cage

Handling hamsters or gerbils regularly from a early age will make them tame, but this does not mean that they will not escape given the chance. Before taking your pet out of its cage, you should always make sure that the room is safe. Close all the doors and windows and make sure that there are no other dangers such as open fires or fan heaters. Other pets, especially dogs and cats, should be shut out of the room.

● **Above:** Both hamsters and gerbils will enjoy the chance to explore the world outside their cage. However, this is an ideal opportunity for your pet to escape. If this happens - don't panic. A lost hamster or gerbil can often be encouraged back by the scent of its favourite food (right).

CHECKLIST

What to do if your hamster or gerbil escapes.

- Keep all the doors and window closed.

- Don't dash around after it. It will become frightened and hide under the furniture.

- Kneel or lie on the floor and offer a small piece of food. Allow the hamster or gerbil to eat the food, encouraging it to climb on to your hand at the same time.

- If you cannot find your pet, keep the doors and windows to the room closed and wait till after dark. It will become more active at night and you should be able to hear it moving around.

Questions *and* Answers

How do I handle a difficult hamster which tries to bite when I pick it up?
If a hamster proves to be very difficult, you can pick it up by the scruff of its neck. There are folds of loose skin here and using these will not hurt your pet, nor will it be able to bite you when held this way.

Do hamsters and gerbils need to have their claws cut?
Hamsters and gerbils are both active creatures and spend most of their waking hours scurrying about. All this activity is usually enough to wear down the claws and keep them in trim.
However, if your pet's claws seem to growing at a strange angle or become very long, your pet will find it increasingly difficult to run around normally. In this case, the claws will need to be clipped by a vet.

Are there any diseases which I could catch from handling my pet rodent?
There are diseases which can be spread from rodents to people. These are called *zoonoses*. Thankfully, both hamsters and gerbils which have been domesticated over many generations now, are very unlikely to carry any serious diseases. But, as with all pets, you should always wash your hands after handling them.

● **Opposite:** *Hamsters and gerbils spend most of their waking hours rushing around exploring any interesting object in their path. This endless activity will usually keep their claws in trim.*

44

● **Above:** *A hamster which tries to bite when handled can be picked up by the scruff of the neck. With regular handling, it will become used to you and less likely to bite.*

Breeding hamsters and gerbils

Because of their aggressive natures, hamsters are harder to breed than gerbils which mate quite naturally within their group. Before you allow your pets to breed, you need to be sure that you can find good homes for the young or you may find yourself with too many pets to house and care for properly. A female hamster can have as many as sixteen young, each of which will need a cage of its own.

Introducing hamsters

Two hamsters placed together need to be watched very carefully to make sure they don't fight. Always transfer the larger female to the male's cage, rather than the other way round, and keep a close eye on them. If the female is ready to mate, she will stand still holding her tail upright. The pair should be separated as soon as they have mated or after 20 minutes if they fail to do so. Separate them immediately if they fight badly.

● **Above:** Hamsters can have big litters with up to sixteen young. Before breeding your pet, you must be sure you can find good homes for all the offspring.

● **Above:** *Once they have mated successfully, a pair of gerbils will continue to mate throughout their lives.*

The pregnant hamster

Golden hamsters have one of the shortest pregnancies of all mammals, with females giving birth after 16 days. The pregnant female should be moved to a converted fish tank where there is no risk of her babies slipping through the bars of a cage.

Breeding gerbils

It is usual to keep a male gerbil with two or three females and these can start to breed from about eight weeks old. Once a pair of gerbils have mated successfully, they will continue to do so throughout their lives so you will need to find plenty of good homes for their young. Adult gerbils will often fight new companions so, if you split up a breeding group, you should introduce them in a new tank or cage.

The pregnant gerbil

Female gerbils will be ready to mate every six days and, when breeding, you will need to provide a nesting box. The male may chase the female and drum with his feet for a while before mating. Female gerbils will give birth after 25 days.

Caring for the young

There will be between four and six young in a gerbil litter and no doubt you will be impatient to see the new babies. However, it is very important not to disturb your pet for the first few days after she has given birth. If you do, it is quite likely that she will attack and kill her young.

● *Above:* *These day-old gerbils are completely helpless. You will not see your own gerbil's litter at this stage as it is very important not to disturb the nest.*

The young litter
Both hamsters and gerbils are blind and helpless at birth, but they grow quickly. Gerbils have a covering of hair and their eyes are open by the time that they are a week old.

Leaving the nest
Once their eyes have opened at around 10 days, the young gerbils will come out of the nest and will be feeding on their own at about two and a half weeks. By the time the youngsters are three weeks old, the litter should be moved to a separate gerbilarium before being separated into male and female groups at around six weeks old.

Young hamsters should be weaned at a similar age to gerbils and re-housed alone when they are six weeks old.

The nursing mother

There is no need to provide a special diet for the female when she is rearing her young, except for more fresh fruit and a little bit of cheese or milk for protein. She will drink more water, so it is important to make sure there is plenty of clean water in the drinker at all times.

● *Top: Young hamsters will be feeding on their own by the time they are two to three weeks old and at six weeks old (above), each hamster should be re-housed in a cage of its own. Once a hamster has reached this age, it is likely to fight even its litter mates.*

Questions *and* Answers

Is it true that female hamsters and gerbils can mate again as soon as they have given birth?
This is true in the case of gerbils and so it is a good idea to move the male gerbil to separate housing. If the gerbils do mate straight away, the second pregnancy will be longer, at around 42 days rather than the standard 25 days. This delay allows the first litter to become independent before the second is born.

Golden Hamster females will not be ready to mate again immediately after giving birth, but if the young hamsters die at an early age, then a female will mate straightaway.

I am worried that all may not be well with my young hamsters in the nest. How can I look at them without causing too much disturbance?
If you really have to check the nest, you can use the blunt end of a pencil, but dip it in the litter on the floor first to disguise its scent. Use the pencil to carefully prize apart the covering over the youngsters and then use it to put the material back once you have checked them.

How can I help my hamster raise her young? Does she need any different foods?
There is really no need to provide extra foods for the female when she is rearing her offspring, except for the possibility of fresh fruit. It appears that slices of fresh apple lower the risk of the mother attacking her young.

● *Above:* *After the birth of a litter, the female hamster will not be ready to mate again until her pups are weaned. It is best to allow her a few months to recover between litters.*

● *Above:* *Your pet gerbil will not need special feeding while she is rearing her young. However, you should provide extra water and make sure that she has a regular supply of fresh food to be sure that she is getting a balanced diet.*

51

Exhibiting your pet

It is possible to enter hamsters and gerbils in competitive shows, but there is a big difference between prize-winning animals and the average pet. Show standards are very high and the judges will look for perfection.

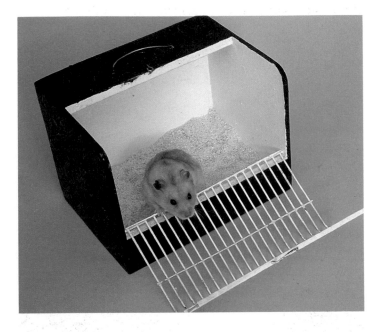

● **Above:** *If you are going to exhibit your pet in shows, you will need to be well prepared for the event. Grooming is important to make sure your pet looks its best and you will need a special show case to house your pet during judging.*

Showing quality

Most of the hamsters and gerbils entered in shows have been specially bred to fit a list of ideals. Ordinary hamsters and gerbils from pet shops are not bred to compete at this level and will often have faults which would be marked down by a judge. A gerbil's ears and eyes may be considered to be small, or a hamster may have uneven markings which means it would have little chance of winning.

Instead, you may prefer to enter your hamster or gerbil in a general pet competition where its friendly character and a well-cared-for appearance hold much more importance.

Showing as a hobby

If you do want to breed hamsters and gerbils to exhibit as a hobby, you will need to start with a show-quality breeding pair. Joining a club and buying specialist magazines are the best ways to find out information about up-and-coming shows and how to prepare for them.

● **Below***: Entering your hamster or gerbil in a show or pet competition can be an exciting event. Only show-quality animals have a real chance of winning in specialist shows, but an ordinary pet can do well in a general pet show.*

Going on holiday

Since gerbils and hamsters are easy to look after, it is not usually difficult to arrange for a friend or relative to care for your pet while you are away. If this is not possible, many boarding kennels that take cats and dogs will also look after small pets of this type. You should arrange for someone to look after your pet as soon as you know when you are going to be away.

Leaving a list

Before going away, you should check that you have enough food and bedding to last for the whole of your holiday. Clean out your pet's cage thoroughly and write out a clear list of instructions for feeding and care of your pet. The easiest way to do this is to set out what needs to be done each day, so that whoever is looking after your pet can simply follow a daily routine.

Providing spare equipment

It is also a good idea to leave a spare water bottle in case the container breaks. If you are going to be away for a long time, you also need to include a suitable brush to clean out the inside of the bottle and the spout.

Transporting your pet

You can take your pet to its temporary home in its cage, but you must make sure that this is secure so there is no risk of your hamster or gerbil escaping during the journey. Never leave your pet in a car on a hot summer's day, even for a short period of time. The temperature inside a car can become extremely hot and your pet could quickly develop heat exhaustion which can be fatal.

● **Opposite:** *Small creatures such as hamsters and gerbils can be taken to their temporary homes in their cages. Check that the cage is secure and there is no chance of your pet escaping before you set off.*

CHECKLIST – Going on holiday

- Arrange for someone responsible to care for your pet as soon as possible.

- Check that you have enough food and bedding.

- Clean out your pet's cage.

- Write a clear list of feeding and care instructions.

- Write down your vet's name and number and the name and age of your pet.

The first signs of illness

Both hamsters and gerbils are usually very healthy animals and, provided that they are kept clean and well-fed, they should not become ill. With regular handling, you will come to know your pet well and should be able to spot any changes or early signs of illness. The time you spend handling your pet is a good opportunity to check that it is healthy.

Consulting a vet
Always consult a vet if you are worried that your pet is sick and never attempt to treat colds or other symptoms yourself. A sick gerbil should be separated from the colony to avoid infecting the others and to make it easier for you to keep an eye on it.

Early signs of illness
Spotting the early signs of illness can often improve your pet's chance of a full recovery. A change in eating habits may be a first warning that all is not well, but bear in mind that a hamster may carry favourite foods to its nest in its cheek pouches and eat them there rather than the food in its bowl.

Impacted pouches
Hamsters may suffer from *impacted pouches* caused by storing unsuitable food or other objects in the pouches in their cheeks. If your hamster has a constant puffy-cheeked look, it will need to be checked by a vet and have the blockages removed.

Wet tail
The droppings will also show if your pet is becoming sick. Diarrhoea may simply be caused by eating too many greens, but it may also show an illness called *wet tail* which affects hamsters. If this is the case, the fur around the base of the tail will become stained and the hamster will lose its appetite. Wet tail is most likely to strike young hamsters and can be difficult to treat.

Colds

Sneezing, especially combined with a runny nose, may be caused by a cold. Alternatively, it may simply be that the bedding has caused a temporary irritation which leads to repeated sneezing for a brief period. The hamster or gerbil should be kept warm and its condition monitored. If it doesn't improve after a day or so, or it appears to be getting worse, a vet should be contacted without delay.

Loss of fur

Both gerbils and hamsters may suffer from loss of fur. This is often a sign of ageing, although it can be caused by injury or be a symptom of *mange*. Surface injuries caused by fighting can be bathed with a mild antiseptic, applied with cotton wool.

● *Above:* A change in appetite may be the first sign that your pet is not well. When you re-fill the food bowl each day, check that the previous day's food has been eaten.

● **Above:** *As your hamster or gerbil grows older, the condition of its coat may change. It may become thinner, duller and may lose patches of fur altogether. However, these can also be signs of illness and a check-up is recommended.*

● **Above:** *Although fur loss can be a symptom of old age or fighting, if the skin appears to be sore or scaly, it is more likely to be caused by an infection, mange or by lice or mites. Each of these conditions is easily treated by a vet.*

Questions *and* Answers

What should I do if I accidentally drop my hamster or gerbil?
Hamsters and gerbils are delicate creatures and can suffer badly if they are dropped or have a fall. After a fall, your pet should be gently returned to its nest and left to recover from the shock. If it doesn't seem to have recovered after an hour, or if you are worried that it has broken bones or internal injuries, you should contact a vet immediately.

Can internal injuries and diseases be treated in pets which are so small?
It is not usual to operate on small pets such as hamsters and gerbils, but thanks to modern anaesthesia it is now possible. A younger animal has a better chance of a full recovery than an older pet.

Some of my gerbils have lost their whiskers. How can I stop this?
One or more of your colony is likely to be biting the whiskers of the other gerbils. This is an inherited trait but may also be a sign of overcrowded living conditions. If the situation does not improve within larger housing, you may need to separate the culprit. The animal responsible will be easy to spot as eventually it will be the only one with a full set of whiskers.

How do I clean a cage which has housed an infected animal?
To make it safe, the cage should be dismantled and thoroughly disinfected before being used to house another animal.

CARE CHECKLIST

DAILY

What to do Add new food, removing any uneaten fresh food which could start to rot. Check for this in the hamster's nest.

Provide fresh water.

Provide a little fruit or greenstuff.

What to look for Check the amount of food that has been eaten.

Check the drinker for any leaks.

Wash all fruit or greenstuff first to remove any harmful chemicals.

WEEKLY

What to do Clean out the cage and add new bedding and lining.

Replace any dirty or badly worn gnawing blocks.

Wash out the water drinker with a bottle brush.

Check supplies of food and buy further supplies if stocks are low.

What to look for Look for any signs of gnawing on the sides of the cage and repair if necessary.

MONTHLY

What to do   Strip down the cage and wash it thoroughly. Make sure it is dry before placing new bedding in the base.

Check your pet's claws are not overgrown and arrange clipping if necessary.

About my pet

MY PET'S NAME IS

MY PET'S BIRTHDAY IS

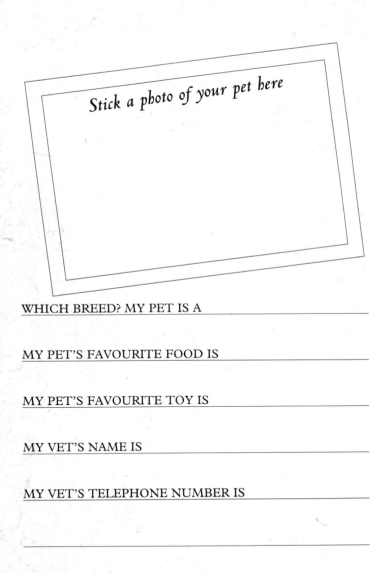

Stick a photo of your pet here

WHICH BREED? MY PET IS A

MY PET'S FAVOURITE FOOD IS

MY PET'S FAVOURITE TOY IS

MY VET'S NAME IS

MY VET'S TELEPHONE NUMBER IS

Index

Agouti (gerbil), **20**
Albino (hamster), **17**
Angora (hamster), **18**
Argente (gerbil), **21**

bedding material, **30, 34, 37**
behaviour, **12-13, 15**
biting/nipping, **14, 40, 44**
Black Mongolian (gerbil), **12**
breeding, **12, 46-47, 50, 53**
buying a pet, **4, 12**

cage, **28**:
  cleaning the, **34-35, 59**
  fitting out, **30-33**
  letting the pets out of, **42**
  positioning the, **36**
care checklist, **60-61**
checking on a litter, **50**
checklist:
  care, **60-61**
  escapes, **43**
  food, **39**
  holiday care, **55**
cheek pouches, **13**
Chinese hamsters, **8, 19, 22**
choosing the right gender, **24-25**
choosing your pet:
  gerbil, **14, 15, 20-21, 22**
  hamster, **14, 15, 16-19, 22**
cleaning the cage, **34-35, 59**
coat:
  gerbil, **20, 22, 58**
  hamster, **18, 19, 22, 58**
colony (gerbil), **9, 12, 29**
colours:
  gerbil, **20-21**
  hamster, **14, 16-19**
Cream (hamster), **16**

daily care, **4, 34, 60**
Dark Golden (hamster), **16**
Domestication:
  gerbils, **11**
  hamsters, **10**
dropping your pet, **59**
Dwarf Russian (hamster), **8, 19, 22, 28**

Egyptian (gerbil), **9**
escapes, **42-43**
exercise wheel, **28, 31**
exhibiting your pet, **52-53**

feeding, **37, 38-39**;
  during rearing, **49, 50**
fish tank, **28-29, 47**
floor covering, **30, 34**
food dishes, **32, 35**
fur, **15, 17, 20, 22, 41**;
  loss of, **57, 58**

gerbilarium, **29, 34**
gnawing, **12, 28**
gnawing blocks, **32**
Golden (hamster), **8, 10, 16**
grooming, **22, 41**

handling, **14, 40, 44, 56**
hibernation, **27**
holiday care, **54-55**
housing:
  gerbils, **29, 37**
  hamsters, **12, 22, 28-29, 37**

illness, **56-57**
introducing a new hamster, **22**

litter of babies, **35, 48, 50**
Long-haired (hamster), **18, 22, 41**

making the room safe, **42**

males and females, separating of, **48**
markings, **18, 22**
mating, **46, 47, 50**
Mongolian (gerbil), **9, 11, 20, 21**

nesting box, **47, 48, 50**

picking up your pet, **40, 41**
playing dead, **13**
pregnancy, **47, 50**

questions and answers:
  breeding, **50**
  care, **44**
  choosing a pet, **22**
  health, **59**
  housing, **37**

Rex (hamster), **18**

Satin (hamster), **18**
sawdust, **30, 35**
'self-coloured' (hamster), **18**
sick animals, **56, 59**
storing food (hamster), **13**

tail (gerbil), **20, 27, 41**
taming, **40**
Tortoiseshell (hamster), **18**
toys, **32, 33, 35**
transporting your pet, **54**
tubular housing, **29, 37**

vet, **26, 44, 56, 57, 59**

White-bellied Golden (gerbil), **21**
wild:
  gerbils, **6-7, 26, 27**
  hamsters, **6-7, 12, 26**
wood shavings, **30**

young animals, **14**;
  caring for, **48-49, 50**